HEAR GOD SPEAK YOUNG CHILDREN

LISTEN

CHELSEA KONG

© 2021 Chelsea Kong

All rights reserved. All images used in this book are licensed copies from their respectful owners including Freepik. This book or any portion thereof may not be reproduced or used in any manner whatsoever without the express written permission of the publisher except for the use of brief quotations in a book review.

Printed in 2021, Made in Toronto, Canada
ISBN: 978-1-7775796-9-2
Library and Archives Canada

Just to say thanks for downloading my book,
please click to get a free books here:
https://chelseak532002550.wordpress.com/contact/

God wants us to hear Him.

Isaiah 6:8
Then I heard the voice of the Lord, saying, "Whom shall I send, and who will go for Us?" Then I said, "Here am I. Send me!"

Teach the little children how to hear God.

God can show them many things.

They will know Him and walk in His ways.

God's Word

Read it.

Think about it.

Write it.

Speak it and do it.

Be with God

Be alone.

Be quiet.

Think of God.

Be Ready

Have a book.

Wait on God.

Write it down.

Draw it on paper.

Be Quiet

Listen to Him.

Let God talk to you.

Be still.

Have Faith

Believe you hear Him.

Believe His Word.

He will speak.

See Jesus with you

He will come to you.

Talk to Jesus.

Tell Him all that is in your heart.

See Him talking to you.

Wait for God to talk

Give God time to talk.

Be quiet to hear.

You can lie down, sit, kneel, or stand.

God gives us

Pictures

Dreams

Visions

Ideas, people, places, things, and invisible things.

Words about the future, past, and present.

How He speaks

A still small voice.

A clear voice like Daddy.

The Bible.

Through others.

Feelings

He also speaks

Words in your head.

Dance

Song

Art

Game

Record it

Write it.

Draw

Dance

Act

Sing

Remember what He said

Think about it.

Keep it in your heart and mind, hear it, and see it.

Do it.

Pray in faith

Pray to God, Jesus, and Holy Spirit.

Keep praying for it and God will act.

Angels will help us.

Do it

Do what God, Jesus, and Holy Spirit says.

Do what daddy and mommy says is right.

Do what the Bible says.

Church and people must do what the Bible says.

Tell Others

Let others know what He says.

Check if it is what the Bible says.

Your family and friends need to know.

God may tell you what to say to them.

God may speak through others.

Practice it

Listen to God every day.

You will hear Him more and He will tell you more.

You know God more and can help others.

Prayer to have Jesus in us

God, I did wrong. Forgive me for my wrong. I believe Jesus Christ died on the cross for me. He rose from the grave to give me His long life. Come into my heart to be my Lord and Savior. I choose to turn away from all wrong. I want to follow you. Help me to walk with you. Keep me safe and teach me. Stop all bad things in my life. Close those doors. Holy Spirit fill me now in Jesus name. Amen.

Be full of the Holy Spirit

Jesus, fill me with Your Holy Spirit. Holy Spirit, come into my life and fill me. Make me full of You. Come with your fire too. Thank you for Your gift to speak Your words in Jesus name. Amen.

Open your mouth and say what God gives you. Ask God what it means. Let Him talk with your mouth. Do it every day to let it grow. You will be closer to Him. Jesus will be close to you. You will have His power. You will do great things and know more.

Prayer

Father God, I want to be close to you. Help me to wait for you to tell me what to do. Jesus, I want to know you. Please open my ability to hear, see, and know you. I want to feel you. I want to be close to you. Teach me your word and to walk with you. Holy Spirit show me more. Be with me all the time. Keep me safe. I want to help others. Bless me in Jesus' name. Amen.

Message from the Author

It is God's plan for children to hear Him so that they can know Him. When they hear God, they will build a relationship with Him. He will teach them and they will grow mature. They will also be close to Jesus and the Holy Spirit. This also helps them to know His plan in their lives and to lead their steps. There are many benefits when they hear Him. It can also save them from danger.

Chelsea Kong Biography

She is a writer, creative arts and digital media artist, and skilled Administrative professional. She is a graduated from Hotel and Restaurant Management, Digital Media Arts, and Office Administration. She also serves in her local church in a variety of roles, from audiovisual, photography, to assisting on the worship team, and ministry team. She also has a passion for families being united. Her writing comprises children's books, stories, bridal writing, poems, lyrics for songs, words of encouragement, blessings, prayers, and jokes. She is the author of the Bridal Collection, Knowing God, How to Hear God's Voice, New Life in Jesus, Loving Israel, God's Gifts, Word Power, Fruit of the Spirit, The Tabernacle, Bride for Jesus, etc. She also has her own Bible Puzzle books and other inspired products. She has a podcast channel called Chelsea K on Anchorfm and podcasts on YouTube. She has been on Unity Live Radio and The Lady Tracey Show. She has an article on Woman of God on Reader's Magnet in the Author Lounge. She is highly recommended by A Proud Christian Blog.

Other Products and more

Other Books by the Author:
https://www.amazon.com/chelseakong
https://www.barnesandnoble.com/s/Chelsea%20Kong
https://www.kobo.com/ca/en/search?query=Chelsea+Kong
https://www.smashwords.com/profile/view/chelseakk8

Podcasts:
https://www.youtube.com/channel/UCOvw9wUmkE08Akeq2z3TQVA

Website:
https://chelseak532002550.wordpress.com

Book Reviews

More books on Amazon, Kobo, and Barnes and Noble, Smashwords, and IngramSpark.
https://chelseak532002550.wordpress.com/

More books on Amazon, Kobo, and Barnes and Noble, Smashwords, and IngramSpark.
https://www.amazon.com/author/chelseakong

Please leave a review and share with friends to help the author continue to write more books to reach more readers. Thank you so much for your support.

Review!

www.ingramcontent.com/pod-product-compliance
Lightning Source LLC
Chambersburg PA
CBHW041415010526
44107CB00016B/1180